Three Little Kittens

Illustrated by Susan T. Hall

Troll

For Hershey, Cowboy, and Mokie

Printed in Canada.   ISBN 0-8167-7464-1

10 9 8 7 6 5 4 3 2

Three little kittens

lost their mittens.

They began to cry.
"Oh, Mother dear,
see here, see here.
Our mittens
we have lost."

"What, lost
your mittens?
You naughty kittens.
Now you shall have no pie."

"Meow, meow, meow, meow.

Now we shall have no pie."

The three little kittens
found their mittens.

They began to cry.
"Oh, Mother dear,
see here, see here.
Our mittens
we have found."

"What, found your mittens?
You're good little kittens.
Then you shall have some pie."

"Purr, purr, purr, purr.

We shall have some pie."

The three little kittens

put on their mittens
and ate up all the pie.

"Oh, Mother dear,
see here, see here.

Our mittens
we have soiled."

"What, soiled your mittens?
 You naughty kittens!"
 Then they began to sigh.

"Meow, meow, meow, meow." They began to sigh.

The three little kittens
washed their mittens . . .

. . . and hung them out to dry.

"Oh, Mother dear,
see here, see here.

Our mittens we have washed!"

"What, washed your mittens? You're good little kittens! Now you may have more pie."

"Purr, purr, purr, purr.
We'll eat up all the pie!"